Table of Contents

Strategy -1...5

Strategy-2 11

Strategy-3 17

Strategy 4................... 22

Strategy -5 26

Strategy-6 30

Strategy -7 34

Strategy-8 38

Strategy 9..42

Strategy -10..46

Strategy-11...50

Strategy-12...54

Strategy-13...57

Strategy-14...61

Strategy-15...65

Strategy- 16..68

Strategy-17...71

Strategy-18...74

Strategy-19...77

Strategy-20...80

Chapter 21 Pro Tips for all Trading set-ups discussed....83

Mastering the Art of Intraday Trading Strategies

Are you intrigued by the fast-paced world of intraday trading, where lightning-fast decisions and market savvy can yield significant rewards? If so, this guide is your essential companion. Dive into 20 proven intraday trading strategies that go beyond basic chart patterns, helping you navigate markets with precision and capture those fleeting intraday opportunities.

Why These Strategies Work: Understanding the "Why" Behind the "What"

We'll blend technical analysis, market psychology, and a hint of fundamental awareness for powerful results. Many of these strategies combine classic indicators, technical tools, and price action patterns in innovative ways. However, rote memorization won't cut it. Successful intraday trading demands real understanding – the "why" behind the setup. That's precisely what you'll gain from this guide!

The Backtesting Imperative: Build Confidence, Minimize Risk

"Hope" is not a trading strategy. That's why backtesting is a recurring theme throughout this guide. Before risking a single dollar in the live markets, historical testing offers a powerful advantage. It validates your strategies, provides a statistical edge, and allows you to refine your execution under various market conditions. The confidence to pull the trigger in real-time comes from the knowledge you've built through extensive backtesting.

Trading Psychology: Your Greatest Weapon (or Your Worst Enemy)

It's easy to get caught up in charts and indicators, but what about the most important factor – your mind? Intraday trading can be exhilarating and stressful in equal measure. We'll discuss the common psychological pitfalls like fear, greed, and hesitation – and how to overcome them. A disciplined, focused mindset is your key to consistent results.

Risk Management: Protecting Your Path to Success

Trading is inherently risky. Preserving your capital isn't just smart – it's essential for long-term survival and growth as an intraday trader. We'll cover the fundamentals of risk management and the importance of developing a strategy that aligns with your risk tolerance and profit goals.

It's About More Than Just the Strategies

Think of this guide as your toolkit for intraday success. The 20 strategies are your powerful weapons, but it's your skill, discipline, and understanding of the markets that make them truly lethal. That's why we delve into the bigger picture of intraday trading!

Charting Your Course: The Power of TradingView

I want to specifically acknowledge TradingView as an indispensable resource for any serious trader. Their platform seamlessly combines advanced charting tools, a vibrant community, and exceptional ease of use. The charts you'll see showcasing our strategies wouldn't be possible without their incredible software. If you haven't explored TradingView yet, now's the time.

Your Journey Starts Now

Ready to unleash your intraday trading potential? This guide marks the beginning. Prepare to see the markets through a seasoned trader's eyes. You'll learn to analyze like a pro, build unshakable confidence, and develop the risk awareness to stay one step ahead. Consider this guide your roadmap to the ever-evolving world of intraday trading – let's explore those strategies and turn your potential into tangible profits!

Strategy 1 - The Holy Grail Strategy

In the dynamic world of intraday trading, the search for reliable, profitable strategies is a constant quest. Today, we'll examine a powerful contender: the 10 and 30 Exponential Moving Average (EMA) crossover strategy, bolstered by the strategic use of red and green bar cancellations. Could this technique be the key to unlocking consistent intraday success? Let's dive in and find out!

The Foundation: 10 EMA & 30 EMA Crossovers

At the heart of this strategy lies the interaction between two Exponential Moving Averages (EMAs). Let's solidify our understanding:

- **Understanding EMAs:** Unlike traditional Moving Averages (MAs) that give equal weight to all price data in a set period, EMAs emphasize recent price action. This responsiveness makes them ideal for intraday traders who want to identify and capitalize on short-term trends with greater clarity.

- **Interpreting the Signals:** A bullish crossover occurs when the faster 10 EMA climbs above the slower 30 EMA, suggesting a potential shift towards upward momentum. Conversely, a bearish crossover signifies a possible trend reversal downward, with the 10 EMA dipping below the 30 EMA.

The Power of Red and Green Bar Cancellations

While EMA crossovers offer directional signals, seasoned intraday traders know that not all crossovers are created equal. This is where red and green bar cancellations come into play, providing a vital layer of confirmation to strengthen our trades. Let's dissect this critical element:

- **Red Bar Cancellation (Bullish Setup):** Imagine the following scenario: The 10 EMA crosses bullishly above the 30 EMA, indicating potential buying pressure. However, before jumping in with a long position, we wait for a red (bearish) bar to form on the price chart. This red bar acts as a temporary pause, allowing us to assess if the bullish momentum holds. If the very next candle after the red bar is green (bullish) and decisively breaks above the high of the red bar, it suggests a strong surge in buying pressure, confirming the initial bullish signal from the EMA crossover. Only then do we enter a long position, feeling more confident in the potential upside.

- **The Green Bar Cancellation (Bearish Setup)**

This concept mirrors the red bar cancellation but for bearish scenarios:

- **Green Bar Cancellation (Bearish Setup):** After a bearish crossover (10 EMA dips below the 30 EMA), we wait for a green (bullish) bar to form. This green bar represents a temporary pause in the downtrend. We only enter a short position (selling) if the very next candle after the green bar is red (bearish) and decisively breaks below the low of the green bar. This confirms the continuation of the downtrend signaled by the EMA crossover.

Why Red and Green Bars?

Let's explore the specific reasons why red/green bar cancellations offer such valuable insights:

1. **Filtering Out False Breakouts:** Not all EMA crossovers are accurate. Sometimes, a brief upward spike in price can trigger a false bullish crossover, or a momentary downward blip can trigger a misleading bearish crossover. The red/green bar cancellations act as filters, allowing us to see if the initial bullishness/bearishness can overcome temporary counter-pressure.

2. **Gauging Market Sentiment:** The red/green bar cancellations also provide a snapshot of the immediate battle between buyers and sellers. If the market can't sustain the initial bullishness from the crossover, a red bar may form. If it can't sustain the initial bearishness after a crossover, a green bar might appear. By waiting for a decisive break above/below these bars, we gain additional

confirmation that the tide is truly turning in the direction of our trade.

Your Trading Playbook

Let's translate this concept into actionable steps:

- **Entry (Bullish):** 10 EMA crosses above 30 EMA, red bar forms, next green candle breaks red bar's high.

- **Entry (Bearish):** 10 EMA crosses below 30 EMA, green bar forms, next red candle breaks green bar's low.

- **Stop Loss:** Initially set at the 30 EMA (at the time of your entry).

- **Partial Profit Booking:** Book some profit when the price is twice the distance between your entry and the 30 EMA.

- **Final Profit Booking:** Close the remaining position if a candle closes below the 30 EMA after you've taken partial profits.

Pro Tips from the Trenches

1. **Ideal Timeframes:** 3-minute and 1-minute charts. Use 1-minute for volatile stocks.

2. **Sweet Spots:** Works well around Pivot Points (PDH, PDL, CPR)

3. **Don't Be Greedy:** Take partial profits as planned!

4. **Respect the Lines:** Avoid this strategy if strong support/resistance levels are against your trade direction.

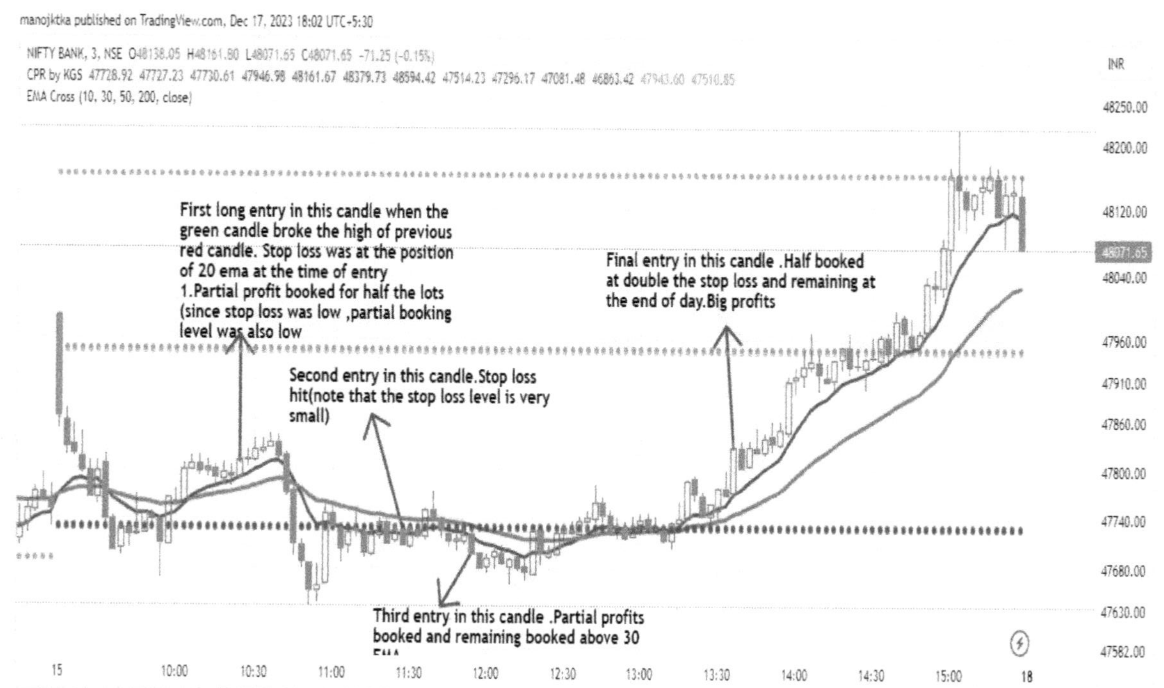

manojktka published on TradingView.com, Dec 17, 2023 18:02 UTC-5:30
NIFTY BANK, 3, NSE O48138.05 H48161.80 L48071.65 C48071.65 -71.25 (-0.15%)
CPR by KGS 47728.92 47727.23 47730.61 47946.98 48161.67 48379.73 48594.42 47514.23 47296.17 47081.48 46863.42 47943.60 47510.85
EMA Cross (10, 30, 50, 200, close)
INR
48250.00
48200.00
48120.00
48071.65
48040.00
47960.00
47910.00
47860.00
47800.00
47740.00
47680.00
47630.00
47582.00
First long entry in this candle when the green candle broke the high of previous red candle. Stop loss was at the position of 20 ema at the time of entry
1.Partial profit booked for half the lots (since stop loss was low ,partial booking level was also low
Final entry in this candle .Half booked at double the stop loss and remaining at the end of day.Big profits
Second entry in this candle.Stop loss hit(note that the stop loss level is very small)
Third entry in this candle .Partial profits booked and remaining booked above 30 EMA
15
10:00
10:30
11:00
11:30
12:00
12:30
13:00
13:30
14:00
14:30
15:00
18
TradingView

Strategy 2-Doji Master

Candlestick patterns offer a visual language for interpreting market sentiment in intraday trading. Among them, the Dragonfly Doji and Gravestone Doji hold particular significance, especially when they appear at crucial support or resistance levels. Let's learn how to strategically leverage these patterns for timely entries and exits.

Decoding the Dojis

- **Dragonfly Doji: The Bullish Signal** This distinctive 'T'-shaped candlestick has a long lower shadow (tail) with little to no upper shadow – a hallmark of buying pressure overcoming selling pressure after an initial dip. When found at support, it hints at a potential bullish reversal.

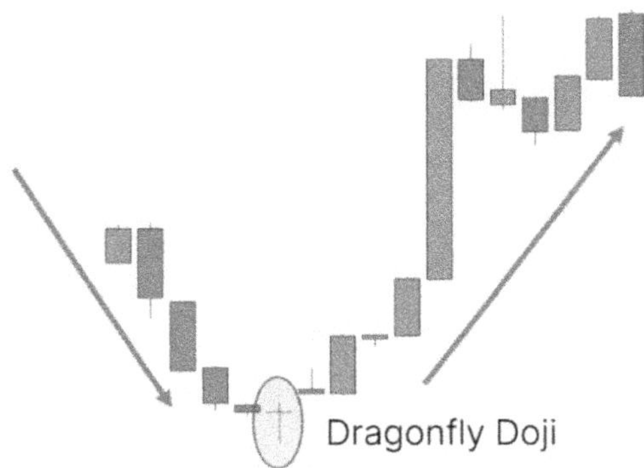

- **Gravestone Doji: The Bearish Warning** The inverted 'T' shape with a long upper shadow and minimal lower shadow signals sellers pushing the price down after an initial surge. Its appearance at resistance suggests a potential bearish reversal.

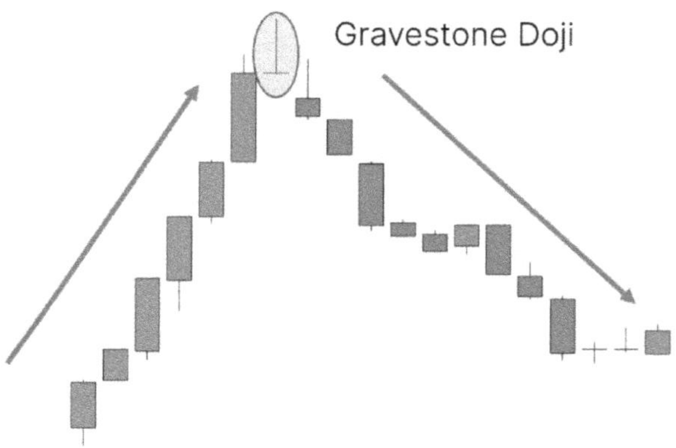

The Importance of Support & Resistance

- **Support:** A price floor where buying pressure tends to halt a downtrend. Think of it as the buying zone.

- **Resistance:** A price ceiling where selling pressure may stall an uptrend – consider it the selling zone.

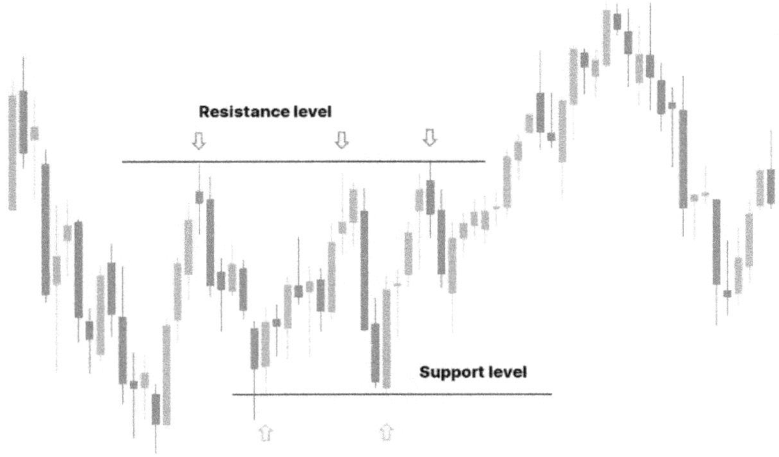

Putting it into Practice

Let's translate these patterns into intraday trading strategies:

Dragonfly Doji at Support

- **Spot the Setup:** Look for a Dragonfly Doji forming at a well-established support level.

- **What it Means:** Selling pressure weakens at support, buyers might be stepping in.

- **Entry:** Wait for a bullish green candle after the Doji. Enter a long position if that green candle closes above the Doji's high.

- **Stop Loss:** Place your stop loss below the Doji's low (or below support if the Doji didn't break it).

- **Exit**: Aim to exit at the next significant resistance or pivot point.

Gravestone Doji at Resistance

- **Spot the Setup**: Look for a Gravestone Doji forming at a clear resistance level.

- **What it Means**: Buying pressure possibly weakens at resistance, sellers might be taking over.

- **Entry**: Wait for a bearish red candle after the Doji. Enter a short position if the red candle closes below the Doji's low.

- **Stop Loss**: Place your stop loss above the Doji's high (or above resistance if the Doji didn't break it).

- **Exit**: Aim to exit at the next significant support or pivot point.

Pro Tips from the Trenches

1. **EMA Check**: If the 20 EMA is close and against your trade direction, consider skipping the setup.

2. **Sweet Spot**: 5-minute charts work best for these patterns.

3. **Early Bird Advantage:** This strategy often shines in the early trading session.

4. **Hidden Barriers:** Even without a recent trend, whole numbers ending in "00" or "50" can act as 'psychological' support/resistance levels.

manojktka published on TradingView.com. Dec 24, 2023 16:05 UTC-5:30
Nifty 50 Index, 5, NSE O21343.40 H21343.60 L21328.45 C21332.35 -11.75 (-0.06%)
EMA Cross (5, 20. 50, 200, close)
INR
21480.00
21440.00
21424.40
21390.00
21350.00
21332.35
21310.00
21270.00
21230.00
21200.00
21170.00
21140.00
21108.00
enter when the next candle
goes above this candle.
Stop loss at the low of DOJI
its a bounce from 20 EMA ,so
high probability set up
14:00
15
11:00
12:00
13:00
14:00
18
11:00
12:00
13:00
14:00
TradingView

Strategy 3-Triangle Breakout with confirmation

Want to spot high-potential breakout opportunities within the day? The Triangle and 20 EMA strategy is your tool. This strategy harnesses the power of triangle chart patterns and the confirming signal of the fast-reacting 20 Exponential Moving Average (EMA) to identify breakouts in either direction. Let's break it down.

Understanding the Strategy

- **The Core Idea**: Find potential breakouts in price trends using triangle patterns, then use the 20 EMA to confirm the direction and strength of that breakout.

Key Components

1. **Triangle Chart Patterns**: Triangles signal a period of consolidation as buyers and sellers battle it out. They come in a few varieties:

   - **Symmetrical**: Hints at an upcoming decision, but the direction is uncertain.

- o **Ascending**: Often a bullish continuation signal.

- o **Descending**: Often a bearish continuation signal.

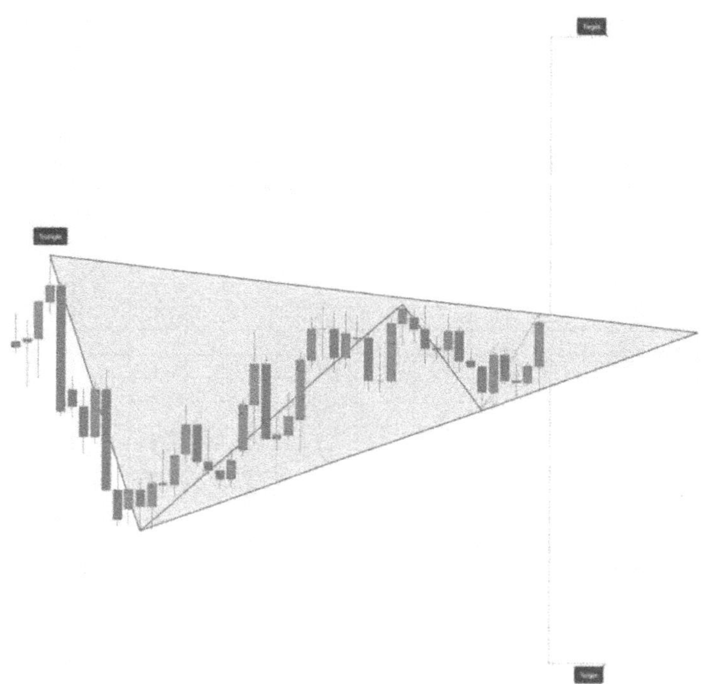

2. **The 20 EMA: Your Confirmation Tool**: This fast-moving average adds another layer of confidence in the breakout's validity:

- o **Breakout Up**: Price breaks above the triangle's upper trendline AND the 20 EMA is also pushing upwards.

- **Breakout Down:** Price breaks below the triangle's lower trendline AND the 20 EMA is also trending down.

Your Intraday Trading Playbook

- **Long Entry:**

  - Price breaks convincingly above the triangle's upper trendline.

  - 20 EMA is trending upwards, confirming bullish momentum.

- **Short Entry:**

  - Price breaks convincingly below the triangle's lower trendline.

  - 20 EMA is trending downwards, confirming bearish momentum.

- **Stop Loss:** Place strategically, considering the recent swing highs/lows that formed the triangle.

- **Exit Strategy:** Take profits when the price hits support/resistance or if a trend reversal signal emerges.

Pro Tips:

- **Timeframes:** This works across timeframes, but intraday traders often find the 5-minute or 15-minute charts ideal.

- **Don't Force It:** If a clear triangle pattern doesn't materialize, don't try to make this strategy fit. Patience is key!

- **Focus on Volume:** Keep an eye on trade volume during the breakout. A surge in volume adds validation to the move.

- **Trend Awareness:** This strategy is more reliable when the breakout aligns with the overall market trend.

manojktka published on TradingView.com, Dec 17, 2023 20:15 UTC+5:30
NIFTY BANK, 5, NSE O48148.65 H48161.80 L48071.65 C48071.65 -70.45 (-0.15%)
CPR by KGS 47728.92 47727.23 47730.61 47946.98 48161.67 48379.73 48594.42 47514.23 47296.17 47081.48 46863.42 47943.60 47510.85
EMA Cross (10, 20, 50, 200, close)
INR
Entry in this candle when
20 EMA came out of
triangle pattern
43880.00
43830.00
43790.00
43750.00
43710.00
43670.00
43630.00
43600.00
43570.00
43540.00
43502.80
35
17
10:00
11:00
12:00
13:00
14:00
14:35
20
10:0
TradingView

Strategy4-Range Breakout of the 3rd 5-Minute Candle after Opening

Intraday trading demands quick analysis and decisive action. The 3rd Candle Range Breakout strategy offers a powerful way to potentially capitalize on those crucial early-morning market moves. Let's see how to use it effectively.

The Significance of the 3rd 5-Minute Candle

- **Setting the Stage:** Those first few candles in a trading day are packed with information. The 3rd candle helps reveal the initial directionality and potential range of the day.

Range Breakout Strategy: The Basics

- **Definition:** Focus on the high and low of the 3rd 5-minute candle to establish a trading range. Look for a breakout above or below these levels for trading opportunities.

Your Intraday Trading Playbook

Bullish Range Breakout

- **Identify the Range:** Note the high and low of the 3rd 5-minute candle.

- **Confirmation:** Wait for price to definitively break above the range's high.

- **Entry:** Consider a long position at the breakout.

- **Stop Loss:** Set it below the 3rd candle's low.

- **Partial Profit Booking:** Target profits three times the range size away (e.g., if the range was $5, aim for a $15 gain).

- **Full Exit:** Close the position if a candle closes below the 20 EMA after taking partial profits.

Bearish Range Breakout

- **Identify the Range:** Note the high and low of the 3rd 5-minute candle.

- **Confirmation:** Wait for the price to definitively break below the range's low.

- **Entry:** Consider a short position at the breakout.

- **Stop Loss:** Set it above the 3rd candle's high.

- **Partial Profit Booking:** Target profits three times the range size away.

- **Full Exit:** Close the position if a candle closes above the 20 EMA after taking partial profits.

Pro Tips

1. **EMA Check:** If the 20 EMA is against your trade direction, consider skipping the setup.

2. **Risk Conscious:** Trade with smaller positions initially, as not every breakout succeeds.

3. **Time is Key:** This strategy is most effective in the early hours of the trading session.

4. **Follow the Trend:** If your breakout direction is against the larger market trend, be extra cautious and seek further confirmation.

5. **Bias Note:** Short trades may have a slightly higher success rate with this setup.

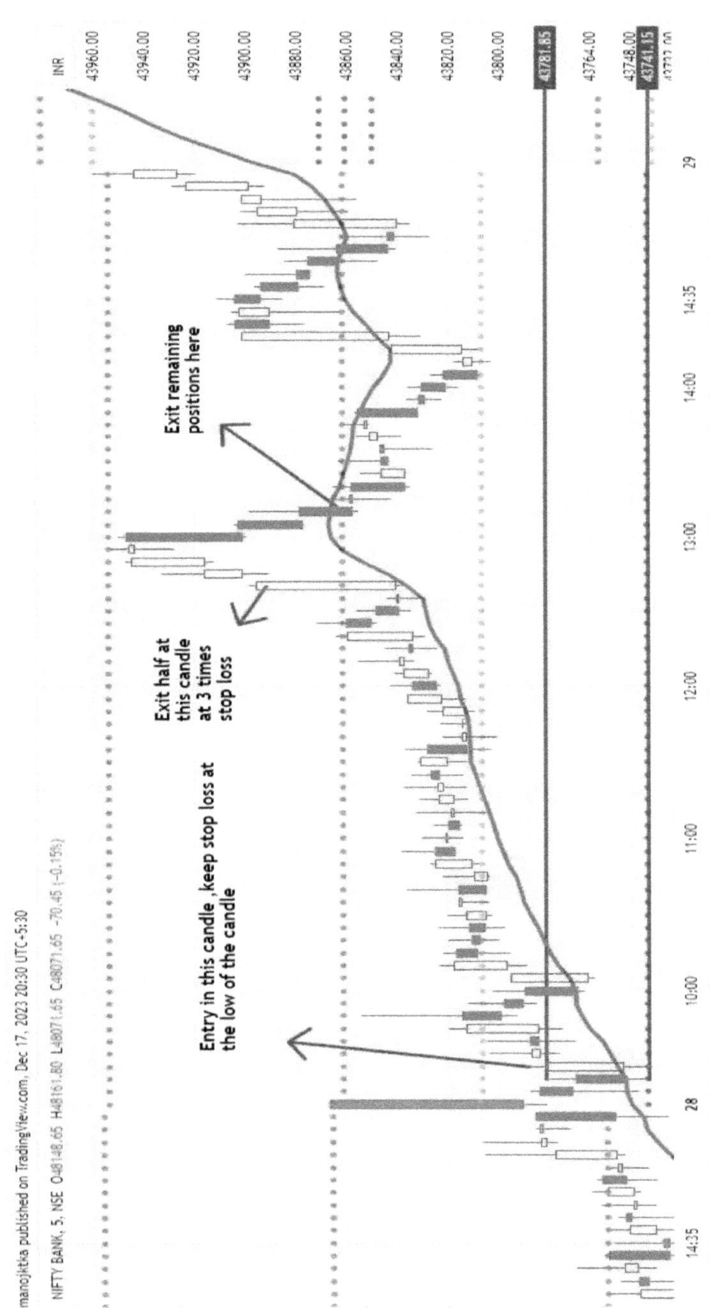

manojjktka published on TradingView.com, Dec. 17, 2023 20:30 UTC+5:30
NIFTY BANK, 5, NSE O48148.65 H48161.80 L48071.65 C48071.65 -70.45 (-0.15%)
Exit remaining positions here
Exit half at this candle at 3 times stop loss
Entry in this candle ,keep stop loss at the low of the candle
INR
43960.00
43940.00
43920.00
43900.00
43880.00
43860.00
43840.00
43820.00
43800.00
43781.85
43764.00
43748.00
43741.15
43723.00
28
10:00
11:00
12:00
13:00
14:00
14:35
29
14:35
TradingView

Strategy 5-Double Top Pattern and 20 EMA

The Double Top pattern is a classic signal of a potential bullish trend running out of steam. Combined with the fast-reacting 20 EMA, it becomes a powerful weapon in the intraday trader's arsenal. Let's see how to use it to spot and take advantage of reversals.

Understanding the Double Top Pattern

- **Definition:** The Double Top looks like an "M" on the chart – the price peaks, pulls back slightly, rallies to roughly the same peak, then starts heading down. This signals weakening bullish momentum and a potential reversal to a downtrend.

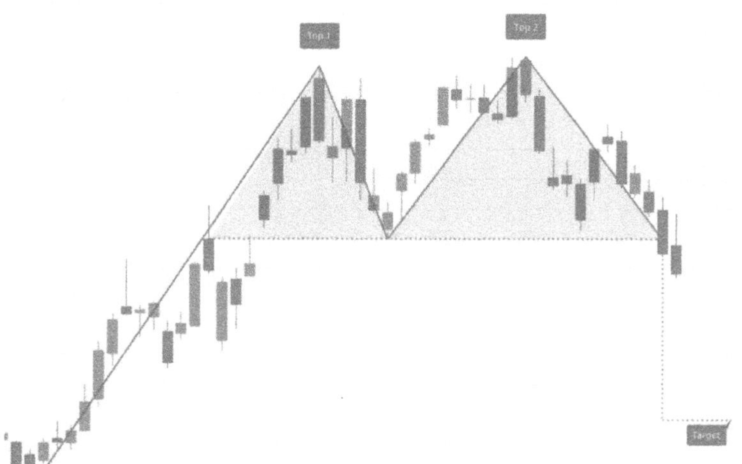

Leveraging the 20 EMA

- **Trend Confirmation**: The 20 EMA helps confirm the trend's direction and strength. In this setup, we want to see the price below the EMA to support the bearish bias of the Double Top.

Your Intraday Trading Playbook

Bearish Double Top Formation

- **Identify the Pattern**: Spot that characteristic "M" shape of the Double Top.

- **20 EMA Check**: Make sure the price is currently below the 20 EMA, suggesting a downtrend.

- **Entry**: Consider a short position when the price convincingly breaks below the neckline (the low point between the two peaks).

- **Stop Loss**: Place your stop loss above the second peak of the Double Top pattern.

- **Partial Profit Booking**: Take some profits when the price drops twice the distance between your entry and the neckline.

- **Full Exit**: Close the position if a candle closes below the 20 EMA after taking partial profits.

Watch Out for Bullish Fakes

- **Caution**: If the price breaks above the second peak of the Double Top, that could signal a bullish fakeout instead. Look to other indicators for confirmation.

Pro Tips

1. **Candle Power**: Large bearish candles after the second top confirm the strength of the selling pressure.

2. **Key Levels**: If the Double Top's peaks align with significant resistance zones (like Pivot Points or PDH), the setup becomes even more reliable.

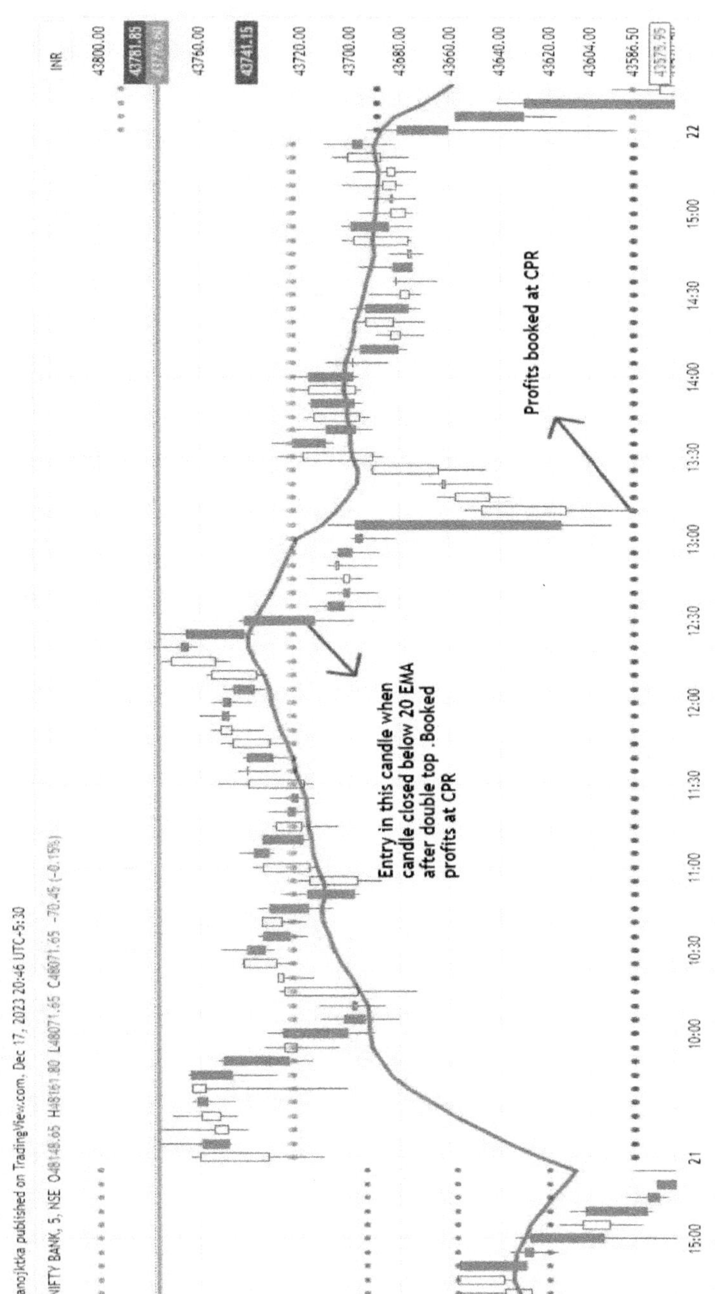

manojktka published on TradingView.com, Dec 17, 2023 20:46 UTC-5:30
NIFTY BANK, 5, NSE O48148.65 H48161.80 L48071.65 C48071.65 -70.45 (-0.15%)
INR
Entry in this candle when candle closed below 20 EMA after double top . Booked profits at CPR
Profits booked at CPR
TradingView

Strategy 6-Three Black Crows Below Resistance

The Three Black Crows candlestick pattern signals a potential bullish trend running out of steam. Its presence below a strong resistance level amplifies its bearish implications and offers intraday traders a high-potential setup. Let's see how to use it.

Understanding the Three Black Crows Pattern

- **Definition:** Three consecutive bearish candles with progressively lower opens, closes, and lows signal weakening buying pressure and increasing momentum to the downside.

THREE BLACK CROWS

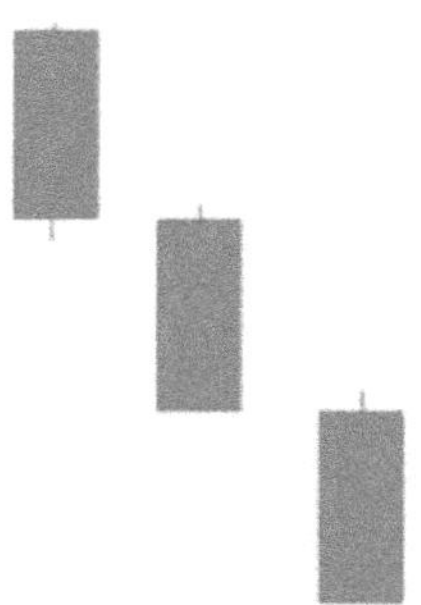

Identifying Resistance Levels

- **What to Look For:** Key areas where sell orders are likely clustered can act as resistance. Consider:

  - PDH, PDL

  - Pivot Points (Standard, Fibonacci, etc.)

  - Psychological round number levels (00, 000)

  - Previously established support/resistance zones

Your Intraday Trading Playbook

Bearish Reversal Below Resistance

- **Spot the Setup:** Observe the Three Black Crows pattern forming right below a clear resistance level.

- **Entry:** Consider a short position when the third black candle closes below the resistance.

- **Stop Loss:** Place your stop above the highest high of the Three Black Crows, or slightly above the resistance level itself for extra caution.

- **Target:** Aim for profits when price reaches the next significant support level or pivot point.

Pro Tips

1. **Volume Check**: High volume during the Crows' formation strengthens the signal.

2. **Timeframe Matters**: This is often an effective short-term strategy, so smaller timeframes may work best.

3. **Await Completion**: Don't enter if the third candle hasn't closed yet.

4. **Trend Check**: If the broader trend is still bullish, be extra cautious; look for other confirming signals.

5. **Don't Force It**: If the setup is unclear, skip it! Patience is key.

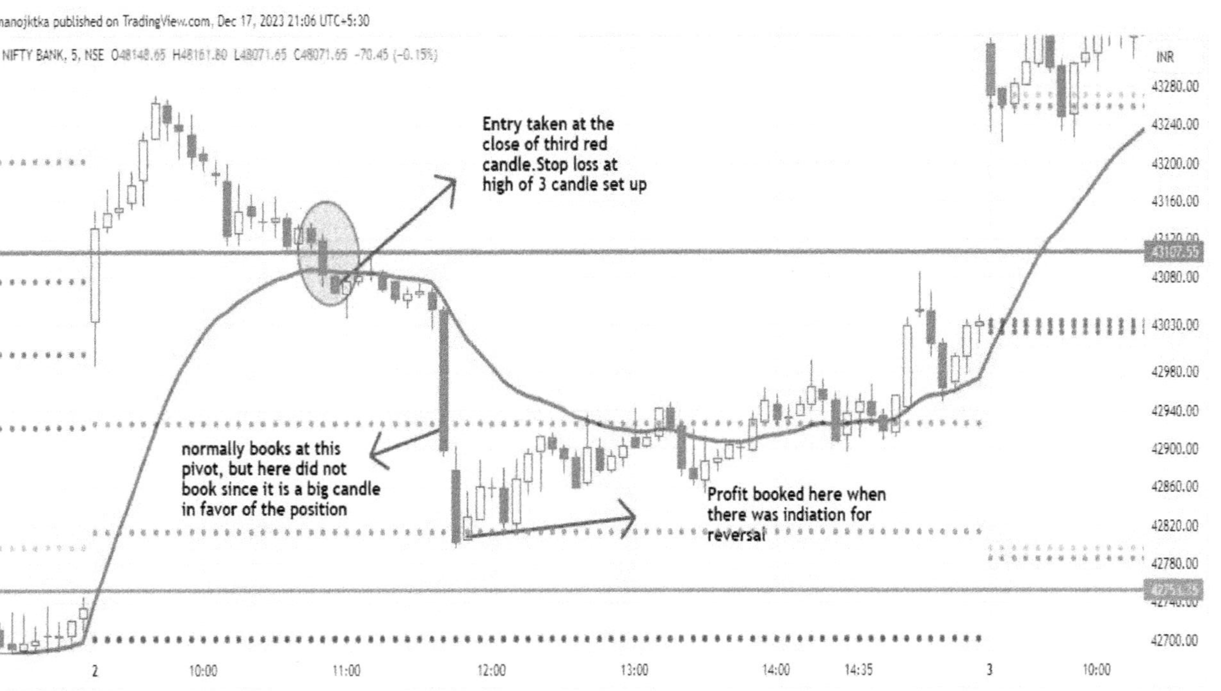

manojktka published on TradingView.com, Dec 17, 2023 21:06 UTC+5:30
NIFTY BANK, 5, NSE O48148.65 H48161.80 L48071.65 C48071.65 -70.45 (-0.15%)
Entry taken at the close of third red candle.Stop loss at high of 3 candle set up
normally books at this pivot, but here did not book since it is a big candle in favor of the position
Profit booked here when there was indiation for reversal
TradingView

Strategy 7-Three White Soldiers
Above Support

The Three White Soldiers pattern is a classic signal of a potential bearish trend reversal. Its presence above a strong support level amplifies its bullish implications and offers intraday traders a high-potential setup. Let's see how to use it.

Understanding the Three White Soldiers Pattern

- **Definition:** Three consecutive, strong bullish candles with progressively higher opens, closes, and highs. This signals increasing buying pressure and a potential momentum shift back to the upside.

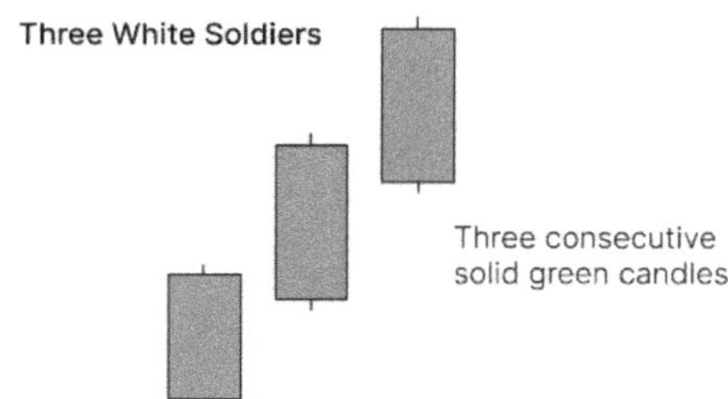

Identifying Support Levels

- **What to Look For:** Key areas where buy orders are likely clustered can act as support. Consider:

  - PDH, PDL

- o Pivot Points (Standard, Fibonacci, etc.)

- o Psychological round number levels (e.g., $100, $200)

- o Previously established support/resistance zones

Your Intraday Trading Playbook

Bullish Reversal Above Support

- **Spot the Setup**: Observe the Three White Soldiers pattern forming right above a clear support level.

- **Entry**: Consider a long position after the third white candle confirms by closing above the support.

- **Stop Loss**: Place your stop below the lowest low of the Three White Soldiers, or slightly below the support level for extra caution.

- **Partial Profits**: Take some profit when the price rises twice the distance between your entry and the low of the pattern.

- **Full Exit**: Close the position when the bullish momentum wanes, such as when a candle closes below the 20 EMA or when price reaches a significant resistance level.

Pro Tips

1. **Volume Check**: High volume during the Soldiers' formation strengthens the signal.

2. **Candlestick Size**: Large white candles make the pattern even more convincing.

3. **Look Back**: Ideally, the recent downtrend was fairly strong, making the reversal more likely.

4. **Trend Check**: If the broader trend is still strongly bearish, be extra cautious; look for other confirming signals.

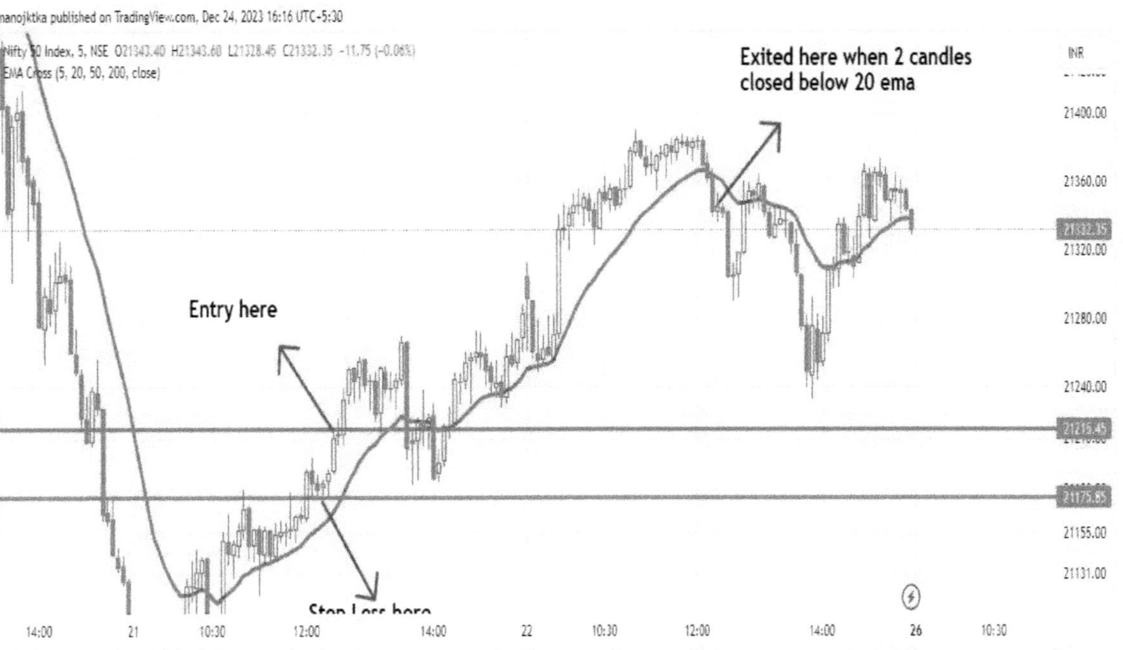

manojktka published on TradingView.com, Dec 24, 2023 16:16 UTC-5:30
Nifty 50 Index, 5, NSE O21343.40 H21343.60 L21328.45 C21332.35 -11.75 (-0.06%)
EMA Cross (5, 20, 50, 200, close)
Exited here when 2 candles closed below 20 ema
Entry here
Stop Loss here
INR
21400.00
21360.00
21332.35
21320.00
21280.00
21240.00
21215.45
21175.85
21155.00
21131.00
14:00
21
10:30
12:00
14:00
22
10:30
12:00
14:00
26
10:30
TradingView

Strategy 8-Gap Open Strategy with Second 5-Minute Candle

Gaps between the previous close and today's open can signal strong momentum...but which way? The second 5-minute candle is key to deciphering the intraday direction. Let's see how this works.

Understanding the Gap Open Strategy

- **Definition**: Trading based on a significant price difference between the previous day's close and the current day's opening price.

Why the Second Candle Matters

- **Post-Open Volatility**: The first 5-minute candle is often chaotic as the market reacts to overnight news.

- **The Second Candle: Clarity**: The second candle often provides a clearer directional signal, helping confirm whether the gap will be filled or if further momentum will play out.

Your Intraday Trading Playbook

1. **Spot the Gap**: Look for a sizable price gap (up or down) at the market open.

2. **Mark the Range:** Note the high and low of the second 5-minute candle. This establishes a potential trading range.

3. **Entry:**

   o **Long:** If price breaks above the second candle's high, consider a long position.

   o **Short:** If price breaks below the second candle's low, consider a short position.

4. **Stop Loss:**

   o **Long:** Place your stop below the second candle's low.

   o **Short:** Place your stop above the second candle's high.

5. **Profit Targets**

   o **Partial:** Consider taking some profits if the price moves twice the distance of the second candle's range.

   o **Full Exit:** Close the position when price hits significant support/resistance or if a candle closes below the 20 EMA.

Pro Tips

1. **Volume Check:** High volume after the gap adds confidence to the move.

2. **Gap Size:** Bigger gaps often indicate greater potential momentum.

3. **Don't Force It:** If no clear gap or strong direction emerges, stay out of the market.

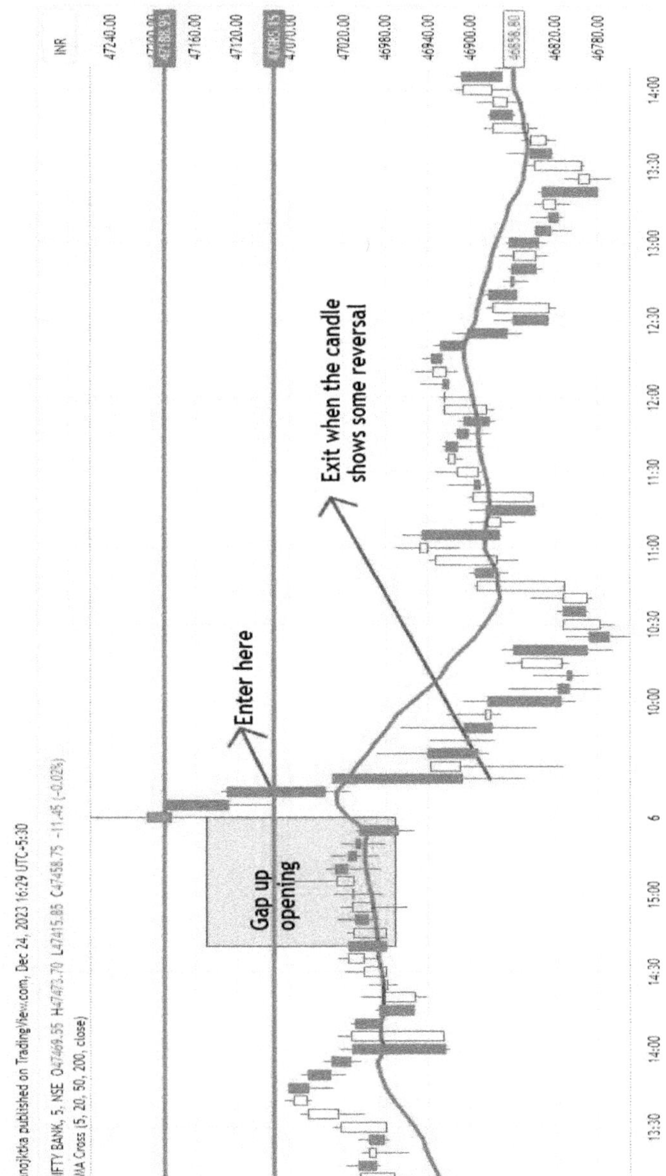
manojitbia published on TradingView.com, Dec 24, 2023 16:29 UTC-5:30
NIFTY BANK, 5, NSE O47469.55 H47470.70 L47415.85 C47458.75 -11.45 (-0.02%)
EMA Cross (5, 20, 50, 200, close)
INR
Enter here
Exit when the candle shows some reversal
Gap up opening
TradingView

Strategy 9-Big Candle Breakout Strategy

Big Candles signal big moves, often fueled by institutional traders entering the market. Spotting these breakouts and acting decisively offers intraday traders a high-potential advantage. Let's harness the power of Big Candles!

Understanding the Big Candle Breakout Strategy

- **Definition:** Trading breakouts either above the high or below the low of a "Big Candle".

- **What is a Big Candle?** It's a single candle that dwarfs the 8-10 candles before it by breaking their highs or lows. This sudden, large movement suggests serious buying or selling pressure.

Why Institutions Matter

Big Candles often indicate institutional traders (banks, hedge funds, etc.) are piling in. Their massive trades add fuel to the breakout fire.

Your Intraday Trading Playbook

1. **Spot the Big Candle:** Look for a candle that takes out the highs or lows of at least the last 8-10 candles.

2. **Confirmation:** Wait for a price break above the Big Candle's high (for a long trade) or below its low (for a short).

3. **Entry:**

   - **Long:** Buy when the price breaks above the Big Candle's high.

   - **Short:** Sell when the price breaks below the Big Candle's low.

4. **Stop Loss:**

   - **Long:** Place your stop below the Big Candle's low.

   - **Short:** Place your stop above the Big Candle's high.

5. **Exiting Your Trade**

   - **Ride the Momentum:** If another Big Candle forms in the same direction as your trade, hold on! The move may have legs.

   - **Exit on Slowdown:** Exit when momentum wanes (smaller candles, lower volume, indicators turning), or when price reaches a significant support/resistance level.

Pro Tips

1. **Downward Moves**: Big bearish candles often trigger stronger breakouts than bullish ones.

2. **Big but Not Too Big:** Genuinely massive candles may be tougher to trade - consider placing your stop loss near the middle of the candle in those cases.

3. **Forget Everything Else:** This strategy defies broader market trends and any other trading strategies - if the setup's there, take it!

1.

manojktka published on TradingView.com, Dec 24, 2023 16:34 UTC+5:30
NIFTY BANK, 1, NSE O47444.25 H47473.70 L47434.85 C47458.75 +14.45 (+0.03%)
INR
Entry here when big candle is formed and subsequent candle broke the low of big candle.See the fall that followed
TradingView

Strategy 10-Flag Breakout and Confirmation

Flag patterns offer a brief pause within a strong trend, followed by a potential breakout continuation in the original direction. Adding a retest confirmation makes this strategy even more reliable for intraday trading.

Understanding the Strategy

- **The Pattern:** Look for a sharp price move (the flagpole), followed by a tight sideways consolidation period (the flag).

- **The Breakout:** Price breaks convincingly above (bullish flag) or below (bearish flag) the consolidation zone.

- **The Retest:** After the breakout, the price often pulls back to retest the breakout level before fully resuming the trend. **This is your entry point.**

Your Intraday Trading Playbook

1. **Spot the Flag:** Look for those visually clear flag patterns – a significant trend followed by a tight consolidation range.

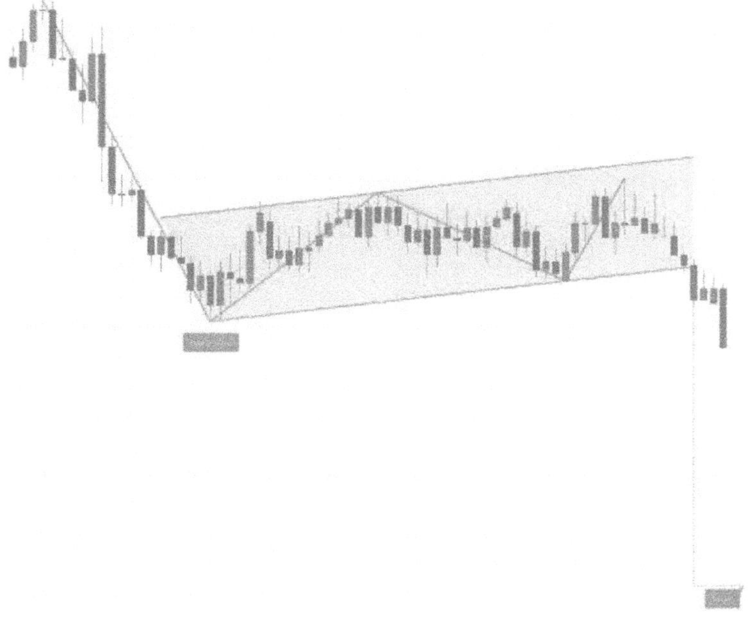

2. **Breakout & EMA:** Wait for the price to clearly break above (bullish) or below (bearish) the flag **and** for the 20 EMA to emerge from the flag zone.

3. **Entry After Retest**

   o **Long:** Buy when the price drops back to retest the top of the flag consolidation and then starts rising again.

   o **Short:** Sell when the price rallies back to retest the bottom of the flag consolidation and then starts dropping again.

4. **Stop Loss:**

- o **Long:** Place your stop below the bottom of the flag pattern, or just below the retest low.

- o **Short:** Place your stop above the top of the flag pattern, or just above the retest high.

5. **Profit Targets**

- o **Partial:** Consider taking some profits when the price moves a distance equal to twice the height of the flag pattern.

- o **Full Exit:** Close the position when price hits significant support/resistance or if trend momentum weakens.

Pro Tips

- **Trend Check:** This strategy works best when the flag forms along with the direction of the broader trend.

- **Pole Height Matters:** The taller the 'flagpole' (the initial move), the more powerful the potential breakout.

manojktka published on TradingView.com, Dec 24, 2023 17:01 UTC+5:30
NIFTY BANK, 1, NSE, O47444.25 H47473.70 L47434.85 C47458.75 +14.45 (+0.03%)
INR
47800.00
47700.00
47600.00
47520.00
47458.75
47440.00
47365.00
47305.00
47245.00
47185.00
47109.75
Entry in this candle ,
the flag is broken and
20 ema came out of
the flag
eventhough the candle come
out of the flag ,no entry made
here because 20 ema is still
inside the flag
13:00
13:15
13:30
13:45
14:00
14:15
14:30
14:45
15:00
15:15
21
09:30
09:45
TradingView

Strategy 11-The CPR + 20 EMA strategy

The CPR (Central Pivot Range) identifies key support/resistance levels. The 20 EMA helps confirm the prevailing trend. This chapter combines them into a straightforward intraday strategy.

Understanding the Strategy

- **CPR: Your Map:** The CPR shows you potential turning points. Imagine the previous day's high, low, and close averaged together, with lines drawn above and below that central point. Those are your CPR levels.

- **20 EMA: Your Compass:** This fast-moving average shows if the short-term trend is up (EMA is rising), down (EMA is falling), or undecided (EMA is flat).

Your Intraday Trading Playbook

1. **Find Your Levels:** Calculate or plot your CPR for the day (TradingView can do this for you).

2. **Check the Trend:** Is the 20 EMA sloping up or down? This tells you the likely direction of the day.

3. **Entry

- **Long:** If price breaks above the upper CPR level **and** the 20 EMA is below the price (trending upwards), consider a long position.

- **Short:** If price breaks below the lower CPR level **and** the 20 EMA is above the price (trending downwards), consider a short position.

4. **Stop Loss:**

- **Long:** Place your stop below the lower CPR level or a recent swing low.

- **Short:** Place your stop above the upper CPR level or a recent swing high.

5. **Profit Targets**

- **Partial:** Consider taking some profits when the price reaches the next major pivot point, or a distance equal to the CPR range size.

- **Full Exit:** Close the position when price hits significant support/resistance or the trend changes (watch the 20 EMA).

Pro Tips

1. When you are using CPR indicator don't use R1 and S1 (which are next pivots below and above CPR) INSTEAD,use PDL and PDH

2. Always book half the positions at PDH or PDL when trades are taken from CPR
3. People says wide CPR means sideways day ,but as per my observation wide or narrow doesn't have much difference .Only treat CPR as a good entry or exit point
4. When you do short positions from PDH always book at TC

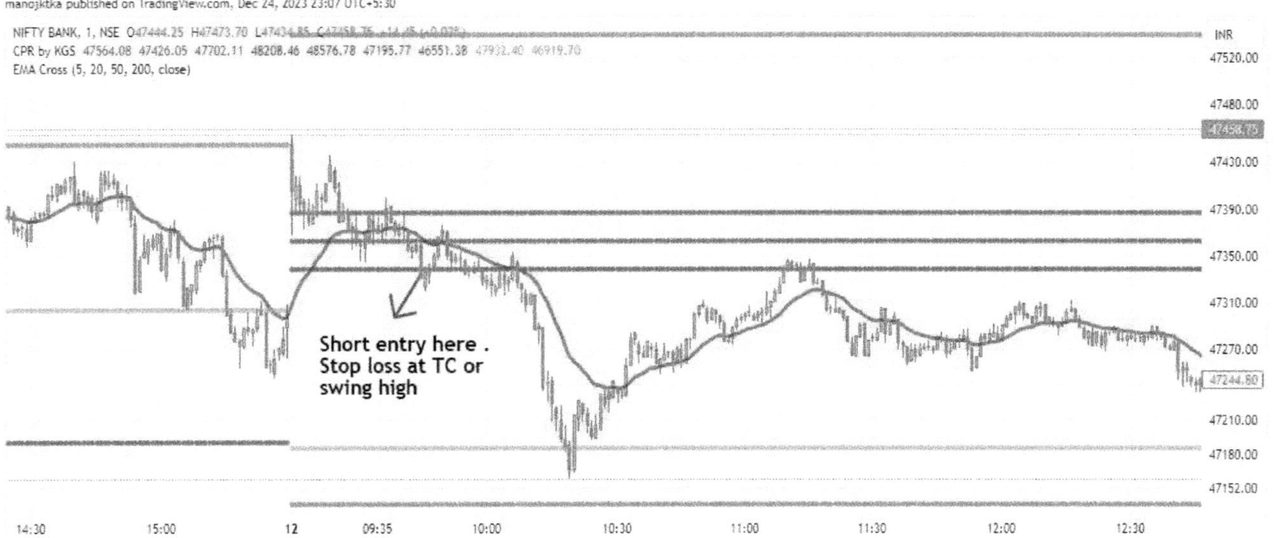

manojktka published on TradingView.com, Dec 24, 2023 23:07 UTC+5:30
NIFTY BANK, 1, NSE O47444.25 H47473.70 L47434.85 C47458.75 +14.45 (+0.03%)
CPR by KGS 47564.08 47426.05 47702.11 48208.46 48576.78 47195.77 46551.38 47932.40 46919.70
EMA Cross (5, 20, 50, 200, close)
INR
47520.00
47480.00
47458.75
47430.00
47390.00
47350.00
47310.00
47270.00
47244.80
47210.00
47180.00
47152.00
Short entry here .
Stop loss at TC or
swing high
14:30
15:00
12
09:35
10:00
10:30
11:00
11:30
12:00
12:30
TradingView

Strategy 12-15 Minute Breakout Strategy (Second 15 minute)

Capitalizing on the 15-Minute Breakout (After the Chaos)

The first 15 minutes of the trading day are often wild. This strategy helps us avoid that volatility and spot cleaner breakout opportunities on the 15-minute timeframe. Let's see how it works.

Understanding the Strategy

- **Why Wait?** The first 15 minutes are full of overnight news reactions, big orders adjusting, and general market confusion. We skip this period to look for more reliable breakouts.

- **The Rules:** Focus on the 15-minute chart. Watch the high and low of the first 15-minute candle...then let the next candle form. **That's** when we look for breakouts.

Your Intraday Trading Playbook

1. **Mark the Range:** Observe the high and low of the first full 15-minute candle after the market open.

2. **Look for Breakouts:** Watch for the price to convincingly break above the high (for a long trade) or below the low (for a short trade) on subsequent 15-minute candles.

3. **Entry**

   o **Long:** Buy when the price breaks above the high of that initial 15-minute candle.

   o **Short:** Sell when the price breaks below the low of that initial 15-minute candle.

4. **Stop Loss:**

   o **Long:** Place your stop below the low of the initial 15-minute range.

   o **Short:** Place your stop above the high of the initial 15-minute range.

5. **Profit Targets**

   o **Partial:** Consider taking some profits once the price moves a distance equal to about twice the range of that first candle.

   o **Full Exit:** Close the position when price hits significant support/resistance or if trend momentum weakens.

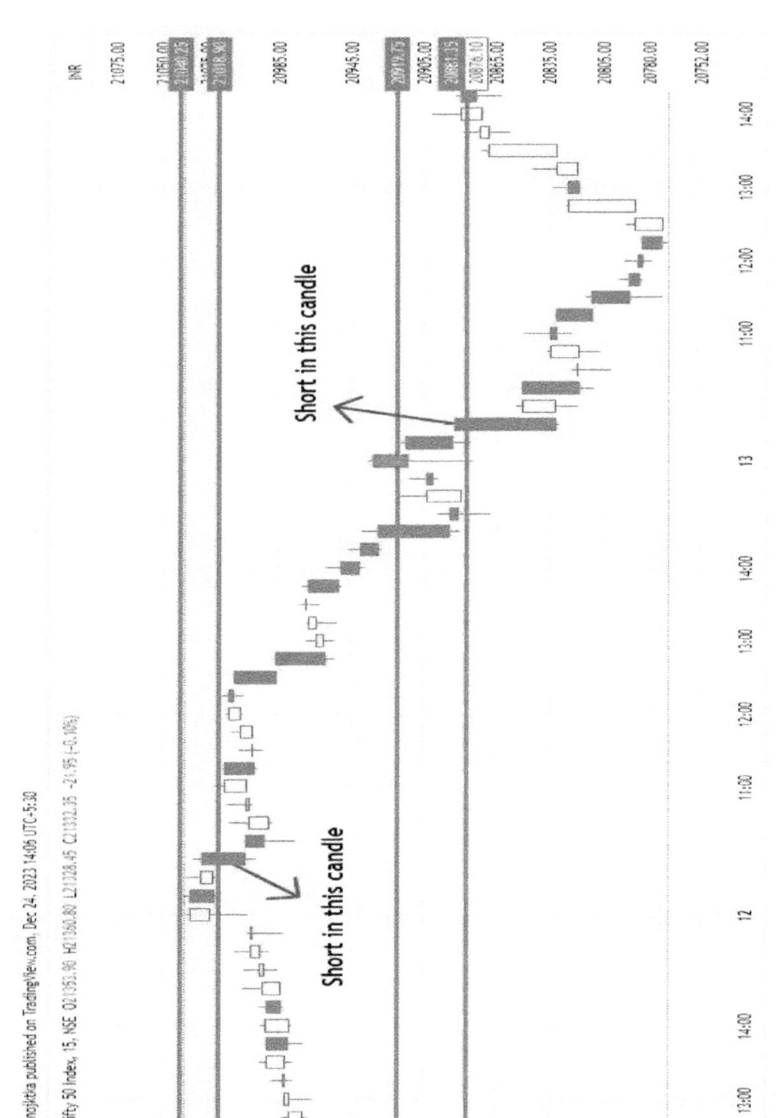

manojixtra published on TradingView.com, Dec 24. 2023 14:06 UTC-5:30
Nifty 50 Index, 15, NSE O21953.90 H21360.80 L21328.45 C21332.35 -21.95 (-0.10%)
Short in this candle
Short in this candle
INR
21075.00
21060.00
21048.75
21018.90
20985.00
20945.00
20919.75
20905.00
20881.35
20876.10
20865.00
20835.00
20805.00
20780.00
20752.00
14:00
13:00
12:00
11:00
13
14:00
13:00
12:00
11:00
12
14:00
13:00
TradingView

Strategy 13-Previous Day High and Evening Star

The Previous Day High (PDH) is a key resistance level. The Evening Star pattern signals a potential bearish reversal. Combining them gives us a high-potential setup for intraday short trades.

Understanding the Strategy

- **PDH: Your Barrier:** The previous day's high point is a natural place where buyers might struggle and sellers might step in.

- **Evening Star: The Reversal Signal:** This three-candle pattern (big bullish, small-bodied, big bearish) suggests bullish momentum is failing, setting the stage for a downtrend.

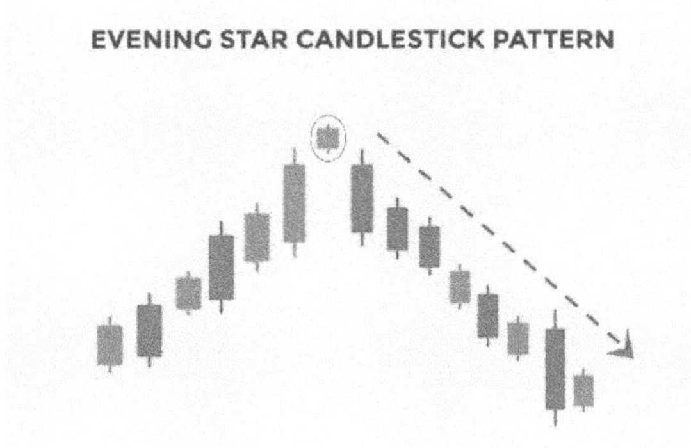

Your Intraday Trading Playbook

1. **Mark the PDH:** Note the previous day's high. This is your potential resistance level.

2. **Watch for the Star:** Look for the Evening Star pattern forming near the PDH. This is your sell signal.

3. **Entry:** Enter a short position when the third candle of the Evening Star closes decisively below the second candle's low.

4. **Stop Loss:** Place your stop above the high of the Evening Star pattern.

5. **Profit Targets**

   o **Partial:** Book half your profits at the CPR (or sooner if it's a huge bearish candle).

   o **Trail the Rest:** Let the remaining position ride, moving your stop loss down to just below each swing low. Close the position if a candle closes above the 20 EMA

<u>Pro Tips</u>

1. Works better in 5 min candle
2. Always book half the position in CPR (if it's a big bearish candle reaching CPR then wait ,look for power slow down)
3. Trail the remaining and book only when candle closes above 20 EMA
4. Look for volume change ,if there is big volume selling then you can add more position once candle closes below CPR

5.

manojktka published on TradingView.com, Dec 24, 2023 23:21 UTC+5:30
Nifty 50 Index, 5, NSE O21343.40 H21343.60 L21328.45 C21332.35 −11.75 (−0.06%)
CPR by KGS 21173.40 21132.58 21214.23 21288.35 20976.80
EMA Cross (5, 20. 50, 200, close)
INR
Short entry here .Stop loss at
evening star high .Book half the
position near CPR and trail the
remaining
21600.00
21550.00
21500.00
21460.00
21420.00
21380.00
21332.35
21310.00
Entry here
21280.00
21250.20
21235.45
14:00
20
10:05
11:00
12:00
13:00
14:00
21
10:05
11:00
12:00
TradingView

Strategy 14-Previous Day Low and Morning Star

The Previous Day Low (PDL) is a key support level. The Morning Star pattern signals a potential bullish reversal. Combining them offers intraday traders a high-potential setup for long trades.

Understanding the Strategy

- **PDL: Your Springboard**: The previous day's low point is a natural place where sellers might struggle and buyers might step in.

- **Morning Star: The Reversal Signal**: This three-candle pattern (big bearish, small-bodied, big bullish) suggests bearish momentum is failing, setting the stage for an uptrend.

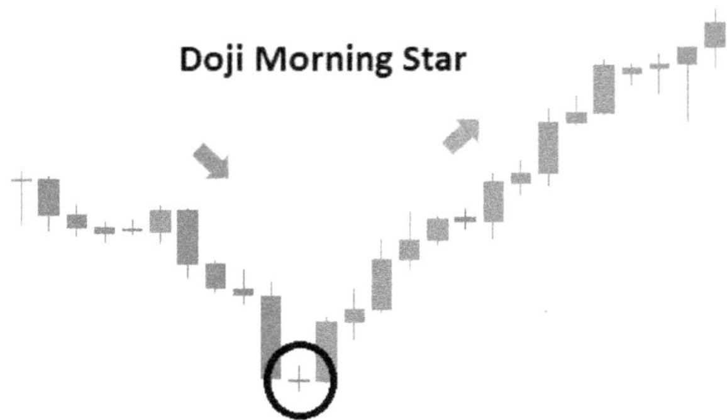

Your Intraday Trading Playbook

1. **Mark the PDL**: Note the previous day's low. This is your potential support level.

2. **Watch for the Star**: Look for the Morning Star pattern forming near the PDL. This is your buy signal.

3. **Entry**: Enter a long position when the third candle of the Morning Star closes decisively above the second candle's high.

4. **Stop Loss**: Place your stop below the low of the Morning Star pattern.

5. **Profit Targets**

- **Target 1:** The CPR (Central Pivot Range) is often a good first target, especially if the third Morning Star candle has good volume.

- **Bigger Moves:** If momentum is strong, consider riding the trade longer. Close the position if a candle closes below the 20 EMA.

manojktka published on TradingView.com, Dec 24, 2023 14:53 UTC+5:30
Nifty 50 Index, 1, NSE O21333.40 H21335.75 L21328.80 C21332.35 −1.55 (−0.01%)
CPR by KG5 21473.40 21132.58 21214.23 21370.00 21484.95 21058.45 20861.85 21388.15 21976.80
EMA Cross (10, 20, 50, 200, close)
INR
21480.00
21470.00
21463.40
21460.00
21450.00
21440.00
21430.00
21420.00
21410.00
21400.00
21388.00
21376.00
21366.00
21356.00
Morning star at PDL and candle closes above 20 EMA very high probability trade
00
10:15
10:30
10:45
11:00
11:15
11:30
11:45
12:00
12:15
12:30
12:45
13:00
TradingView

Strategy 15-Last 30 Minutes Range of Previous Day

The closing action of the previous day often sets the stage for the new trading day. By focusing on the last 30 minutes, we can spot key levels where the intraday battle may be fought.

Understanding the Strategy

- **The Key Levels**: The high and low of the previous day's final 30 minutes become our potential support and resistance zones for the current day.

Your Intraday Trading Playbook

1. **Mark the Range**: Note the high and low of the previous day's last 30 minutes. These are your key levels.

2. **Watch for Breakouts**: If the price breaks convincingly above the high of that range, consider a long trade. If it breaks below the low, consider a short trade.

3. **Entry**

   - **Long**: Buy when the price breaks above the previous day's 30-minute high.

- **Short**: Sell when the price breaks below the previous day's 30-minute low.

4. **Stop Loss:**

   - **Long**: Set your stop below the low of the previous 30-minute range.

   - **Short**: Set your stop above the high of the previous 30-minute range.

5. **Profit Targets** Aim to make at least twice your initial risk (i.e., if your stop loss is 20 points below your entry, try for a 40 point gain). Consider taking partial profits earlier if a key level (Pivot Point, etc.) is in the way.

Pro Tips

- **Trend Check**: This strategy works best when the breakout aligns with the broader trend.

- **Look Back**: Often, the direction of that last 30 minutes gives clues about the likely direction of the next day's open.

manojktka published on TradingView.com, Dec 24, 2023 23:31 UTC+5:30
Nifty 50 Index, 5, NSE O21343.40 H21343.60 L21328.45 C21332.35 −11.75 (−0.06%)
EMA Cross (5, 20, 50, 200, close)
21214.23 21288.35 20976.80
Last 30 mins range of previous day
Short entry here
Candle closes below last 30 mins range of previous day and today is not a gap opening day
TradingView

Strategy 16-20 EMA and Red/Green Bar Cancellation

The 20 EMA helps us confirm the trend direction. Red/green bar cancellations offer us specific buy/sell signals within that trend. Let's see how to use this powerful combination.

Understanding the Strategy

- **EMA: Your Trend Filter**: An upward-sloping EMA suggests an uptrend, a downward-sloping EMA suggests a downtrend. We'll trade with the trend.

- **Red/Green Bars: Reversal Signals**: These bar formations hint at a potential change in momentum that we can exploit.

Your Intraday Trading Playbook

1. **Trend Check**: Is the 20 EMA sloping up (bullish trend) or down (bearish trend)?

2. **Look for Bars**: Wait for a red (bearish) bar to form during an uptrend or a green (bullish) bar during a downtrend.

3. **Wait for Cancellation:**

- **Bullish:** If the next candle's high breaks above the red bar's high, buy.

- **Bearish:** If the next candle's low breaks below the green bar's low, sell.

4. **Stop Loss:** Place your initial stop at the 20 EMA level.

5. **Profit Targets**

   - **Partial:** Book some profits when the price moves a distance equal to twice your initial stop loss distance.

   - **Full Exit:** Close the entire position if a candle closes below the 20 EMA (for longs) or above it (for shorts).

manojktka published on TradingView.com, Dec 24, 2023 14:56 UTC-5:30
Nifty 50 Index, 1, NSE O21333.40 H21335.75 L21328.80 C21332.35 -1.55 (-0.01%)
CPR by KGS 21173.40 21132.58 21214.23 21370.00 21484.95 21058.45 20861.85 21288.35 20976.80
EMA Cross (10, 20, 50, 200, close)
Green bar cancellation below 20 EMA ,short here
Morning star at PDL and candle closes above 20 EMA very high probability trade
TradingView

Strategy 17-20 EMA Mean Reversion

Think of mean reversion like a rubber band. Stretch a price too far in one direction, and it'll want to snap back towards its average. The 20 EMA (Exponential Moving Average) shows us that average, while reversal candles signal the "snap" is about to happen.

Understanding the Strategy

- **The 20 EMA: Your Baseline:**

- The 20 EMA represents the 'normal' price over the last 20 periods. When prices are far from it, that stretch is likely to be unsustainable.

- **Reversal Candles: Your Triggers:** These patterns (dojis, hammers, etc.) show buyers or sellers stepping in after a big move, suggesting a reversal back towards the 20 EMA.

Your Intraday Trading Playbook

1. **Stretch or Shrink:** Look for prices that are unusually far above (for shorts) or below (for longs) the 20 EMA.

2. **Find the Reversal Candle:** Wait for a candlestick pattern that suggests the trend may be weakening

(shooting star at the top, hammer at the bottom, etc.).

3. **Entry**

   - **Long:** Buy when a reversal candle forms after the price has been far below the 20 EMA.

   - **Short:** Sell when a reversal candle forms after the price has been far above the 20 EMA.

4. **Stop Loss:** Place your stop just beyond the swing high/low that the reversal candle formed at.

5. **Take Profits:** Aim to exit at least a portion of the position as the price approaches the 20 EMA. Full exits may be taken when the price crosses the EMA.

<u>Pro Tips</u>

1. If the reversal candles are big candles and it reaches 20 EMA very fast, don't book at 20 EMA, wait till the momentum looses, sometimes it gives big profits
2. If the reversal candle is very big place the SL at half the candle
3. If the reversal happens from crucial support /resistance levels like PDL,PDH,CPR ,then this strategy is very high probability set up

manojktka published on TradingView.com, Dec 24, 2023 15:07 UTC+5:30

NIFTY BANK, 1, NSE O47444.25 H47473.70 L47434.85 C47458.75 +14.45 (+0.03%)
EMA Cross (5, 20, 50, 200, close)

TradingView

Strategy 18-Double top and Gap Up combined

Gap ups can signal overenthusiastic buyers...and set the stage for a harsh reversal. The double top pattern indicates those bulls are losing momentum, offering us a clear shorting opportunity.

Understanding the Strategy

- **The Gap Up:** A big upward gap at the open shows strong buying pressure, often due to overnight news or sentiment shifts.
- **Double Top: The Fading Rally:** Two peaks at roughly the same level, formed after the gap up, suggest the move may be unsustainable and sellers are ready to step in.
- **The Reversal:** When the price breaks below the neckline (the low point between the two tops) it signals the bullish momentum has failed and a downtrend may be starting.

Your Intraday Trading Playbook

1. **Spot the Gap Up:** Look for a sizable upward gap at the market open.

2. **Watch for the Tops:** Wait for the first peak to form, then fall slightly. If a second peak forms at roughly the same price as the first, we have a potential double top.
3. **Confirm the Reversal:** Wait for the price to break convincingly below the neckline - the low point between the two peaks.
4. **Entry:** Sell short when the price breaks below the neckline of the double top pattern.
5. **Stop Loss:** Place your stop loss at the high of the double top pattern.
6. **Profit Targets:** Take partial profits when the price drops a distance at least equal to the gap size. Consider a full exit at significant support levels or if a candle closes above the 20 EMA.

Pro Tips

1. Of all the strategies discussed in this book ,this one gives the biggest returns ,so never miss them

manojktka published on TradingView.com, Mar 24, 2024 16:25 UTC+5:30
Nifty 50 Index, 3, NSE O22078.80 H22093.20 L22076.85 C22080.80 +2.05 (+0.01%)
INR
21850.00
21800.00
21734.60
21720.00
21689.90
21634.95
21576.95
21560.00
21510.00
21460.00
21400.00
21340.00
21290.00
21250.20
21197.00
Gap up and double top
=Big profits
14:30
15:00
23
10:00
10:30
11:00
11:30
12:00
12:30
13:00
13:30
14:00
14:30
15:00
TradingView

Strategy 19-Double Bottom and Gap Down combined

Gaps down can signal panic selling, often overshooting to the downside. The double bottom pattern then indicates those sellers are exhausted, setting the stage for a bullish reversal.

Understanding the Strategy

- **The Gap Down:** A big downward gap at the open shows strong selling pressure, often due to bad news or a bearish shift in market sentiment.

- **Double Bottom: The Buying Begins:** Two troughs at roughly the same level, formed after the gap down, suggest sellers are losing control and buyers are becoming more aggressive.
- **The Reversal:** When the price breaks above the neckline (the high point between the two bottoms) it signals the bearish momentum has faded and an uptrend may be starting.

Your Intraday Trading Playbook
1. **Spot the Gap Down:** Look for a sizable downward gap at the market open.
2. **Watch for the Bottoms:** Wait for the first trough to form, then rise slightly. If a second trough forms

at roughly the same price as the first, we have a potential double bottom.

3. **Confirm the Reversal**: Wait for the price to break convincingly above the neckline – the high point between the two bottoms.
4. **Entry**: Buy when the price breaks above the neckline of the double bottom pattern.
5. **Stop Loss**: Place your stop loss below the lowest point of the double bottom pattern.
6. **Profit Targets**: Take partial profits when the price rises a distance at least equal to the gap size. Consider a full exit at significant resistance levels or if a candle closes below the 20 EMA.

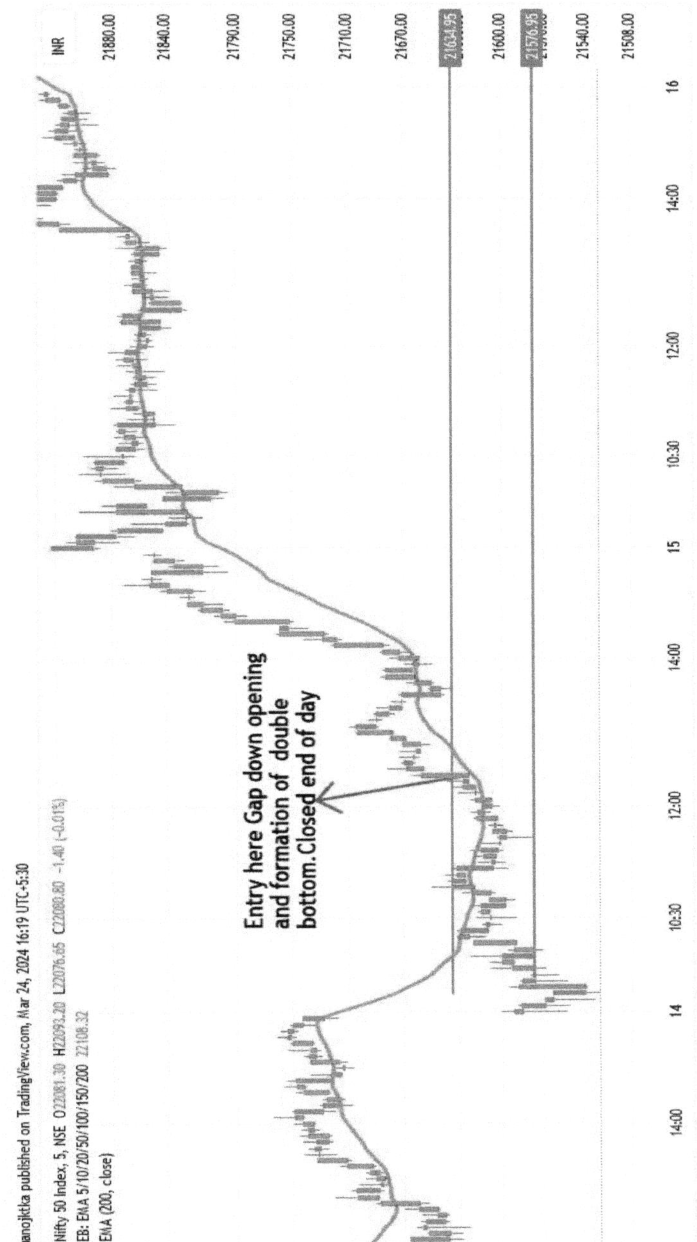

manojitha published on TradingView.com, Mar 24, 2024 16:19 UTC+5:30
Nifty 50 Index, 5, NSE O22081.30 H22093.20 L22076.65 C22080.80 −1.40 (−0.01%)
EB: EMA 5/10/20/50/100/150/200 22108.32
EMA (200, close)
INR
21880.00
21840.00
21790.00
21750.00
21710.00
21670.00
21634.95
21600.00
21576.95
21540.00
21508.00
Entry here Gap down opening
and formation of double
bottom.Closed end of day
14:00
10:30
12:00
14:00
15
10:30
12:00
14:00
16
TradingView

Strategy 20-The Scalper Strategy

Understanding the Scalper Strategy

At its core, the Scalper Strategy revolves around exploiting short-term price movements through the meticulous analysis of candlestick patterns. Whether bullish or bearish, these patterns serve as the cornerstone of strategic entry and exit points, enabling traders to capitalize on rapid fluctuations in asset prices.

Bullish Pattern (Long)

The bullish variant of the Scalper Strategy unfolds across three consecutive candlesticks:

1. Candle 1: A red (bearish) candle sets the stage, signaling a period of selling pressure.
2. Candle 2: A green (bullish) candle emerges, hinting at a potential reversal in sentiment.
3. Candle 3: A green candle that surges above the high of Candle 2 solidifies the bullish outlook.

We must trade as soon as Candle 3 breaches the high of Candle 2, without waiting for the candle to close.

Bearish Pattern (Short)

Conversely, the bearish iteration of the Scalper Strategy capitalizes on potential downward movements:

1. Candle 1: A green (bullish) candle initially dominates, suggesting bullish sentiment.
2. Candle 2: A red (bearish) candle follows, signaling a shift in momentum.
3. Candle 3: A red candle that plummets below the low of Candle 2 confirms the bearish bias.

Stop Loss: Set the stop loss at the respective high or low of Candle 2, depending on the pattern (bullish or bearish).

Target: Aim for a profit target equivalent to three times the stop loss, providing a favorable risk-reward ratio.

Pro Tips

1. Works best in 5 min timeframe
2. Trade in Morning session and evening sessions only

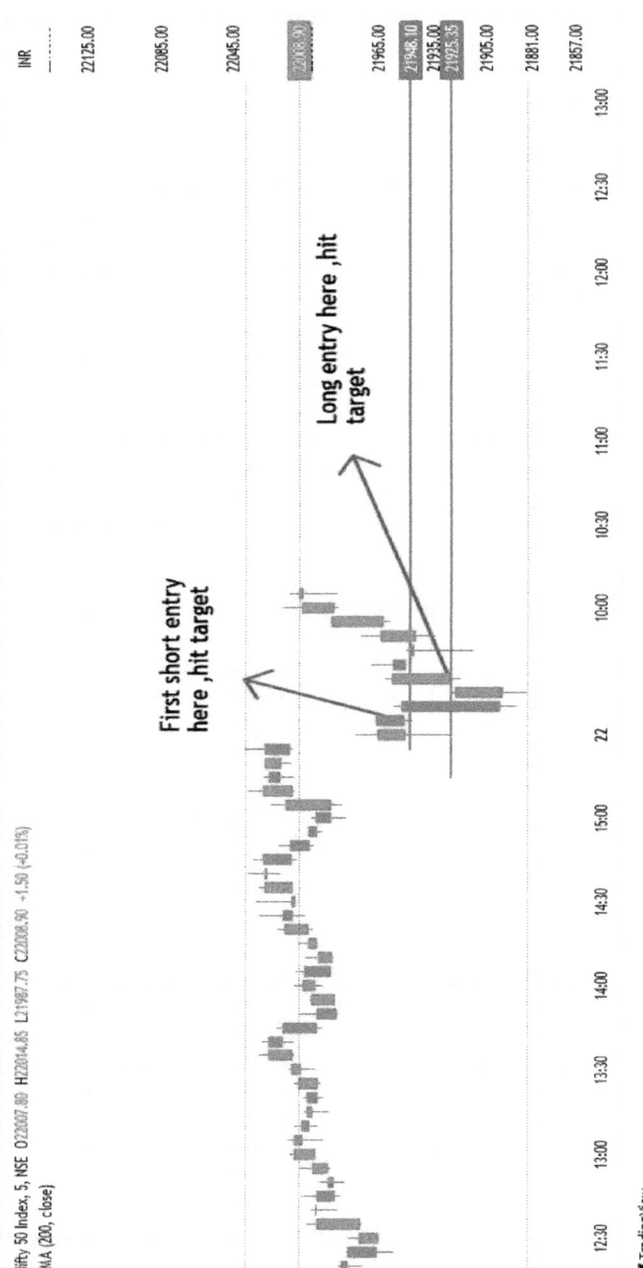

manojktka published on TradingView.com, Mar 24, 2024 16:11 UTC+5:30
Nifty 50 Index, 5, NSE O22007.80 H22014.85 L21987.75 C22008.90 +1.50 (+0.01%)
EMA (200, close)
INR
22125.00
22085.00
22045.00
22008.90
21965.00
21948.10
21935.00
21925.35
21905.00
21881.00
21857.00
First short entry here ,hit target
Long entry here ,hit target
12:30
13:00
13:30
14:00
14:30
15:00
22
10:00
10:30
11:00
11:30
12:00
12:30
13:00
TradingView

Chapter 21 Pro Tips for all Trading set-ups discussed

1. For intraday trading take <u>confirmation from 20 EMA</u> always
2. Always book <u>partial profits</u> above stop loss amount
3. Use <u>time frames</u> depending on the time you are planning to remain on the trade. For scalping 1minute candle works best
4. <u>CPR</u> is one of the most powerful support/resistances
5. <u>Always wait for</u> Pattern Completion
6. Don't follow too many candle stick patterns blindly. Just find some <u>powerful ones</u> and follow that only
7. Keep a tab on <u>institutional</u> activity (check volume and big candles)
8. Before starting a month note down all the major <u>events</u> scheduled to happen in that month, take a note how it may affect the market and trade accordingly (before 1 month is must)
9. <u>Volume</u> gives an early indication

10. Rounded numbers ending with "OOO" and "500" acts as support /resistance
11. Bearish moves are <u>faster</u> than bullish so trade accordingly
12. **<u>Trade what you see not what you think</u>**
13. Note down <u>your mistakes</u> in a book, we often repeat those unknowingly so reading about it will help us minimizing that

Back testing & Tweaking: Leveling Up Your Strategies

So, you've got the Strategies basics – spotting trends, CPRs, all that good stuff. But before throwing real money at it, how do you KNOW it'll shine for YOUR trading style? Enter: backtesting and optimization. Think of it like target practice before the big game.

Why Backtesting is Your Trading Buddy

- **History Repeats Itself...Kinda:** Backtesting lets you replay past charts, seeing how your strategy would have done. Not magic, but helps spot holes or surprising strengths.

- **Find Your Timeframe Sweet Spot:** Strategies work great on daily charts, but maybe YOU kill it on 4-hour? Testing tells you, not guesswork.

Optimization: Small Tweaks, Big Potential

- **One Thing at a Time:** Ditch the kitchen-sink approach. Test adding just ONE filter, or a tighter stop-loss, and see the impact before changing everything.

- **Don't Chase Perfection:** Winning every single "past" trade is misleading. Look for what CONSISTENTLY makes the biggest difference.

- **Test Across Chaos:** Gotta see how the strategy holds up on good days, bad days, and sideways messes. Don't fall for strategies that only work in your ideal perfect world.

Extras to Consider

- **Newsflash!:** Big surprise news messed up a winning trade? Note that when replaying, it wouldn't have been predictable even using the strategy perfectly.

- **Trade Diary + Replay = Growth:** Did you make some impulsive, non-Strategies decisions when looking at past charts? Be honest! Awareness is half the battle.

Here's a Tasty Example

Let's say 60% of your losses hit stop-losses that were WAY far away from the entry. Could going slightly tighter actually give trades breathing room and improve your profits? This is what you'd investigate!

Important Caveats

- **Start Simple, Get Smart:** Optimization gets real tricky if you haven't nailed the basics yet.

- **Paper Trading FTW:** After adjusting, trade without real money for a bit. Testing beats blindly trusting even the best backtests.

Backtesting and optimization are how you become a more strategic trader. It unveils hidden weaknesses, highlights your strengths, and lets you personalize a strategy that's tailored to you. And that's WAY more powerful than trying to copy-paste someone else's setup.

Your Secret Weapon – Journaling for Strategy & Mindset Mastery

The Strategies provides your trading framework, but a detailed journal reveals what's going on inside your head while you apply it. Think of it like an athlete reviewing game footage: painful to watch sometimes, but the fastest way to identify where gains can be made.

Why Write Things Down?
- **Your Brain Lies to You:** We misremember bad decisions, gloss over wins we got lucky on, and invent reasons where none existed. A journal combats this treacherous optimism.
- **Patterns Emerge:** Were you consistently taking trades too early when feeling impatient? Do Mondays make you overconfident? Seeing it laid out gets you closer to solutions.
- **Strategies Spotlights:** Did a setup technically fit your rules, but you hesitated with an underlying gut feeling? That instinct might be worth honing on future setups.

What to Log (Sample)

- **Market Details:** Date/time, symbol traded, brief notes on overall market context (volatile day, bullish news, etc.)

- **The Trade Idea:** Trend direction, CPR levels justifying setup, your planned stop-loss and initial target.
- **Pre-Trade Mindset:** Stressed? Bored? Confident? A one-word emotion check-in reveals A LOT later
- **The Execution:** Did you trade exactly as planned? Any hesitations or rule-breaking to note.
- **Trade Outcome:** Win/Loss is less important than WHY. Luck? Discipline? Or did the Strategies fail completely?

Reviewing for Growth

- **Look for Repetition:** Multiple trades ruined by FOMO? This isn't about beating yourself up, it's about seeing red flags BEFORE they damage your account.
- **Honesty Over Harshness:** You'll make mistakes; the journaling goal is progress, not punishment. Identifying errors lets you devise safeguards moving forward.
- **Strategies Tweaks:** Maybe the strategy requires adjustment for your personality. Should targets be smaller to reduce emotional blowback when they're hit? This awareness improves the strategy itself.

Extra Journaling Power-Ups

- **Screenshots:** Include charts WITH your trade setup drawn in. Sometimes the mistake only becomes obvious visually.
- **Video Journal Alternative:** Struggle with writing? Record yourself talking through trade ideas before you click "buy/sell". Awkward for sure, but revealing about subconscious thinking.
- **Combine with Backtesting:** Noticed fear driving decisions during replay? Now your backtesting has additional angles to focus on.

Key Takeaways

- **Consistency Pays Off:** Daily journaling, even short entries, is more useful than marathon sessions once a month. Habits beat heroic effort.
- **It's NOT All About Trades:** Did you skip proper research due to burnout, or cut a loser early out of panic? Your overall well-being impacts your trading too.
- **There's No "Right" Way:** Find the methods that force YOU to look critically at your trading actions and the thoughts behind them.

From Chaos to Calculated Profits: Why Your Daily Routine is Your Trading Superpower

Imagine starting every single workday without a plan, simply scrambling to address whatever crisis pops up at that moment. Sounds exhausting, right? Yet, many new traders approach the markets with this same kind of disorganized approach – and, unsurprisingly, their results become just as erratic and prone to failure. A solid routine turns you from a reactive novice to a proactive trader in control of their own success.

The Dangers of Trading Without Structure

- **Opportunity Blindness:** Without set times for market analysis, prime setups go unnoticed. When you only half-glance at stressed-out moments, it's all too easy to miss a textbook pattern your method was designed to exploit.

- **The Emotional Rollercoaster:** "Winging it" leaves you open to trading solely based on how you *feel* in the moment. Excitement nudges you into early entries, a recent loss prompts fear and hesitation...this leads to inconsistency and self-sabotage.

- **Learning Curve Flatlines:** Sporadic trading makes it impossible to track progress meaningfully. Was yesterday's loss due to poor execution or a flaw in your overall strategy? With a well-defined routine, results become actionable data!

Why Master Traders Rely on Routines

It's tempting to romanticize trading as this thrilling high-stakes gamble. In reality, the real professionals excel precisely because of their adherence to consistent habits:

- **Time as a Strategic Tool:** Pre-market prep, mid-day check-ins, post-market reviews – each of these becomes a predictable "milestone" in their trading day, optimizing focus and ensuring timely actions when opportunity does strike.

- **Pattern Recognition Mastery:** When watching markets at the same time each day, you start to see how certain setups develop (or fail) at predictable points. Your ability to discern trends, spot reversals, and anticipate likely scenarios improves.

- **Mindset Management:** Trading psychology isn't some fluffy afterthought. Routines instill discipline, helping you remain objective when that wave of fear or greed might tempt you to ignore your rules.

Building Your Own Routine: Customization is Key

Your ideal routine shouldn't turn you into a mindless robot! Here's how to make it a powerful, sustainable tool:

- **Start Simple, Add Depth:** Maybe only commit to 20 minutes of disciplined chart review per day initially. Nail that consistency, then add journaling, strategy backtesting, etc.

- **Life/Trading Harmony:** A 4am routine works for some...disaster for others. Adapt based on natural energy levels and real-life commitments. A routine should optimize your time, not make you miserable.

- **Evolve and Adapt:** A great routine isn't set in stone. Maybe you start focused on chart analysis, later incorporate news review if your strategy involves those types of events. Tweak the process as your trading skills and experience grow.

- **Beyond Just Chart Time:** Consider including elements like:

  - Brief meditation/visualization for calming pre-market jitters

  - Performance tracking: Did you adhere to stop losses? Write it down – both wins and losses provide valuable insight

  - Skill Sharpening: Set aside blocks to revisit educational material, practice on a demo account, or engage in trader community discussions

The Bottom Line

A dedicated routine won't guarantee instant wealth, but it puts you on the right path. Think of it like this: Would you rather face the chaotic, ever-changing world of markets armed with a clear plan and practiced, calculated responses...or stumble around each day, reacting haphazardly, just hoping something works out?

Essential Strategies Trading Rules & Mastering Your Mindset

The Strategies offers your framework, but unwavering discipline and strategic execution make the difference between theory and profit. These rules enhance your Strategies analysis and forge the crucial mindset to stay in the game for long-term success.

Foundation Pillars

1. **Rules Are Your Ruler:** The strategy, your pre-defined risk limits, and trading plan provide structure. When violated, step back and reassess.

2. **Patience Pays:** Wait for candle closes at critical levels, never force trades, and use "no trade" days strategically for observation and learning.

3. **Risk Before Reward:** Position sizing reflects setup strength (stronger = possibly larger, weaker = smaller). Know your non-negotiable stop-loss BEFORE placing an order.

4. **Structure is Supreme:** Analyze the bigger picture using multiple timeframes. Does the overall market context support your planned short or long trade? Fight against, not with, the dominant flow.

5. **Strategies Purity**: Master the core concepts of trend, CPR, and support/resistance before adding unnecessary complexity. Too many indicators slow your decisions.

6. **Partial Profit Protection**: Book some gains near previous swing highs/lows – these act as temporary barriers. Take money off the table while staying active.

7. **Adaptive Risk Management**: Learn the art of trailing stops for some flexibility but avoid being shaken out by normal volatility. Wide, fixed stops limit your potential.

8. **Winners Need Space (Sometimes)**: If a trade breaks significant levels with momentum and maintains strong Strategies signals, it may be profitable to ride a portion longer, protecting profits on the rest.

9. **News = Volatility**: High-impact events derail setups. Consider profit preservation BEFORE surprises happen, or adjust position sizing if you anticipate wild swings.

10. **The Critical Filter**: Impulsive moves often stem from impatience and greed. Ask: Does this trade TRULY meet my core Strategies criteria, or am I succumbing to emotion?

11. **Lessons in Losses**: Analyze losing trades objectively. Are there recurring weaknesses in

your strategy or emotional blindspots? Great traders evolve after mistakes.

12. **Don't Feed the Greed Monster:** Use targets, partial profit-taking, and discipline to combat unrealistic goals. Giving back profits is demoralizing and counterproductive.

13. **Stay Alert on Mondays:** Weekend excitement can create over-eagerness at the week's open. Be especially mindful of impulsive trading during this time.

14. **Honest Foundation:** Success requires brutal self-assessment. Identify weaknesses, seek improvement, and ditch your ego at the door.

15. **Your Instruments, Your Strengths:** Focus on understanding a handful of markets or assets in depth for the best edge.

16. **Adapt or Get Left Behind:** Market conditions change; can your strategy and mindset adjust, or is it best to sit out until conditions suit it?

17. **Buffer for Unknowns:** Unexpected life events happen. Ensure you have some cash cushion outside your actively traded capital to protect your trading journey.

18. **Scaling Up Too Fast**-Early wins tempt larger trades without earned confidence. One bad outcome destroys gains and confidence. Start

small, scale-up systematically based on proven performance.

19. **Continuous Improvement**-Markets, your skills – always evolve. Analyze past trading, seek new concepts, test Strategies optimizations on historical data to stay ahead

20. **Don't Try to Outsmart the Market**-Forcing low-odds setups, expecting your genius overtakes the market – you'll lose. Stick religiously to your clear Strategies criteria; no setup, no trade.

Dear Friends,

I hope you found the strategies in this book helpful. While I would have loved to publish it in color, the cost was prohibitive. However, I have many marked charts that could be useful to you. If you'd like them, please reach out to me at:

20masterstrategies@gmailcom
89219 78807 -WhatsApp

If you found the strategies valuable, I would greatly appreciate it if you could leave a review on the platform where you purchased the book.

As emphasized throughout the book, maintaining a trading journal is crucial for success. I have published a comprehensive trading journal that covers all the essential aspects. I encourage you to purchase a copy and start tracking your trades, as analyzing them is key to improvement. You can find it where you bought this book.

There are four additional high-success-rate strategies that I wanted to include in this book. However, they require extensive examples for proper explanation, so I'll be releasing them later. Please keep an eye out for those, as I believe they offer exceptional probability of success and risk-reward ratios.

If you have any questions regarding the strategies in this book, please don't hesitate to contact me through the details provided above.